BEANS

Life Cycles

ABDO
Publishing Company

A Buddy Book
by **Julie Murray**

VISIT US AT
www.abdopublishing.com

Published by ABDO Publishing Company, 4940 Viking Drive, Edina, Minnesota 55435.

Printed in the United States.

Coordinating Series Editor: Sarah Tieck
Contributing Editor: Michael P. Goecke
Graphic Design: Deb Coldiron
Cover Photograph: MediaBakery.com
Interior Photographs/Illustrations: Corbis, Fotosearch; Media Bakery; Photos.com
Special thanks to the United Soybean Board and the United States Department of Agriculture for use of photos.

Library of Congress Cataloging-in-Publication Data

Murray, Julie, 1969–
    Beans / Julie Murray.
        p. cm. — (Life cycles)
    ISBN-13: 978-1-59928-702-7
    ISBN-10: 1-59928-702-1
    1. Beans—Juvenile literature. 2. Beans—Development—Juvenile literature. I. Title.

SB327.M87 2007
635'.65—dc22

2006034265

Table Of Contents

What Is A Life Cycle?

Beans are living things. The world is made up of many kinds of life. People are alive. So are swans, sheep, bats, and pumpkins.

Beans come in many different shapes, sizes, and colors.

Every living thing has a life cycle. A life cycle is made up of many changes and processes. During a life cycle, living things are born, they grow, and they reproduce. And eventually, they die. Different living things start life and grow up in unique ways.

What do you know about the life cycle of beans?

All About Beans

Beans are a crop that is grown in fields. They are raised in most parts of the world. Beans are a very nourishing vegetable for people to eat. They also have other uses.

Beans are healthy food. They provide protein, iron, and vitamins that our bodies need.

There are many different types of beans. These include snap beans, lima beans, black beans, chickpeas, and soybeans. Each type of bean has a unique taste, use, texture, and appearance.

A Bean Plant's Life

The soybean is one of the most important beans in the world. A soybean plant begins life as a seed. It grows best in sunny, warm places. But, scientists have created soybean plants that grow well in cooler places, too.

The soybean plant's growing cycle begins in spring. Farmers plant seeds when the soil is about 50°F (10°C). Once planted, the seeds sprout and soybean plants begin growing.

Over the summer, the plants grow bigger and bigger. And, they grow leaves. Soon, small blossoms appear near the

Soybean plants grow pods filled with soybeans.

leaves. Then, the blossoms turn into soybean pods. When the plants are fully grown, it is time to harvest their pods.

People can eat harvested soybeans. They can also use soybeans to make important products. Have you ever eaten soybeans?

Guess What?

…Many vegetarians, or people who don't eat animal products, eat foods made with soybeans. This is because soybeans are a great source of protein.

…Soybeans were first grown in China about 5,000 years ago! The emperor considered them a special plant.

People can buy soy milk, soy chicken nuggets, and soy burgers.

Soybean oil is used for cooking.

…Soybeans contain an oil that is used to make many products. Factories crush the seeds to get the oil. It is used in paint, make up, plastic, and ink! Other soybean parts are useful, too. Soybean flakes and meal are fed to animals.

Starting To Grow

Soybean plants are grown in fields. They grow small pods that contain soybeans. These beans are the plant's seeds.

The United States produces the most soybeans in the world. Brazil, Argentina, and China are also top producers.

In the past, farmers used their own beans to start soybean plants. But today, most farmers buy their seeds from seed companies. These seeds grow healthier crops.

The soybean planting process starts in winter. At that time, farmers plan what crops to plant. They also decide which fields they will plant in. Finally, they order seeds.

When the weather is warm enough, planting begins. Most farmers use machines to help them plant soybean crops.

Before planting, some farmers plow and clear the remains of the past year's crop. Then, they plant new seeds in rows.

Other farmers use a method called "no till." These farmers don't plow or remove crop waste. Instead, they drill through it to plant in the soil below. This helps improve soil quality.

Sometimes farmers rotate crops. For example, they plant corn in soybean fields, and soybeans in cornfields. This is because soybeans help make soil richer.

Soybeans take nitrogen from the air and use it to grow. Then, they put nitrogen back into the soil. Corn plants need nitrogen-rich soil to grow. But unlike soybeans they cannot pull nitrogen from the air.

From Seed To Bean

Once planted, soybean seeds germinate in the ground. Soon, tiny soybean plants come up through the soil. Sun and rain help them grow. The plants grow many leaves in all directions.

Small soybean plants will grow to be between 2 and 4 feet (61 and 122 cm) tall.

After six to eight weeks, small purple or white flowers blossom near the base of the leaves. These blossoms become pods. Most soybean plants grow many pods, which look like pea pods. Soybeans grow inside of them.

Ready To Harvest

In early autumn, farmers look for signs that the soybean plants are fully grown. The plants should appear dry and brown. Often, the leaves have fallen off. And, the pods should be gray, brown, or yellow. Then, the soybeans are ready to be harvested.

Farmers used to harvest crops by hand. Today, they use large machines called combines for harvesting.

One combine can help harvest many rows of soybean plants at once.

Soybeans are moved from the field to a truck using equipment such as combines.

A combine separates the pods from the soybean plants. Then, it separates the soybeans from the pods. The soybeans are put into a holding tank. The other parts of the plants are left in the field.

Endings And Beginnings

After harvesting, the soybean plant dies. But, this is not the end of all soybeans. The soybean plant's pods are filled with soybeans. So, it can reproduce.

Every time a farmer plants seeds, it helps create a new generation. This is the beginning of another life cycle.

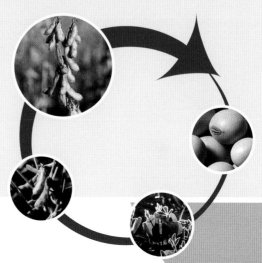

Can You Guess?

Q: What surprising nutrient do soybeans provide?

A: Protein!

Q: What family do beans belong to?

A: Beans are part of the legume family.

Peanuts are one type of legume.

Important Words

generation a group that is living at the same time and is about the same age.

germinate to grow from a seed.

nitrogen an element found in the air and in the earth.

nourish to provide nutrients.

nutrient vitamins and minerals found in food that promote growth and health.

process a way of doing something.

reproduce to produce offspring, or children.

texture the way something feels when touched.

unique different.

Web Sites

To learn more about beans, visit ABDO Publishing Company on the World Wide Web. Web site links about beans are featured on our Book Links page. These links are routinely monitored and updated to provide the most current information available.

www.abdopublishing.com

Index